MALE/FEMALE

BOOKS BY WILLIAM STEIG

About People (1939)

The Lonely Ones (1942)

All Embarrassed (1944)

Small Fry (1944)

Persistent Faces (1945)

Till Death Do Us Part (1947)

The Agony in the Kindergarten (1950)

The Rejected Lovers (1951)

Dreams of Glory (1953)

Male/Female (1971)

William Steig

MALE/FEMALE

Farrar, Straus and Giroux New York

Library of Congress catalog card number: 79-171491
ISBN 0-374-20092-0
Published simultaneously in Canada by Doubleday Canada Ltd., Toronto
Printed in the United States of America by The Murray Printing Company
First edition, 1971
Designed by Janet Halverson

Of the 145 drawings in this book, 21 (some in slightly different form) appeared originally in The New Yorker.

POEM FOR MY BROTHER'S BOOK

How lucky we are
that our planet is not bald like the Moon

that its skin nourishes mushrooms and orchids
and enchambers waters and coals

that serpents find damp joys here
that bulls are made rapturous by cows
and Earth's gown of air carries their bellows

that when at 5 AM the Sun squints
his wild vermilion eye over the rim of the world
the light is gathered by forests of flittering pennons

that no matter the rages of some Ages and some sons
our mothers are born and born again

Arthur Steig

W. Steig

8 BARBERS
IN
ATTENDANCE

W. Steig

W. Steig

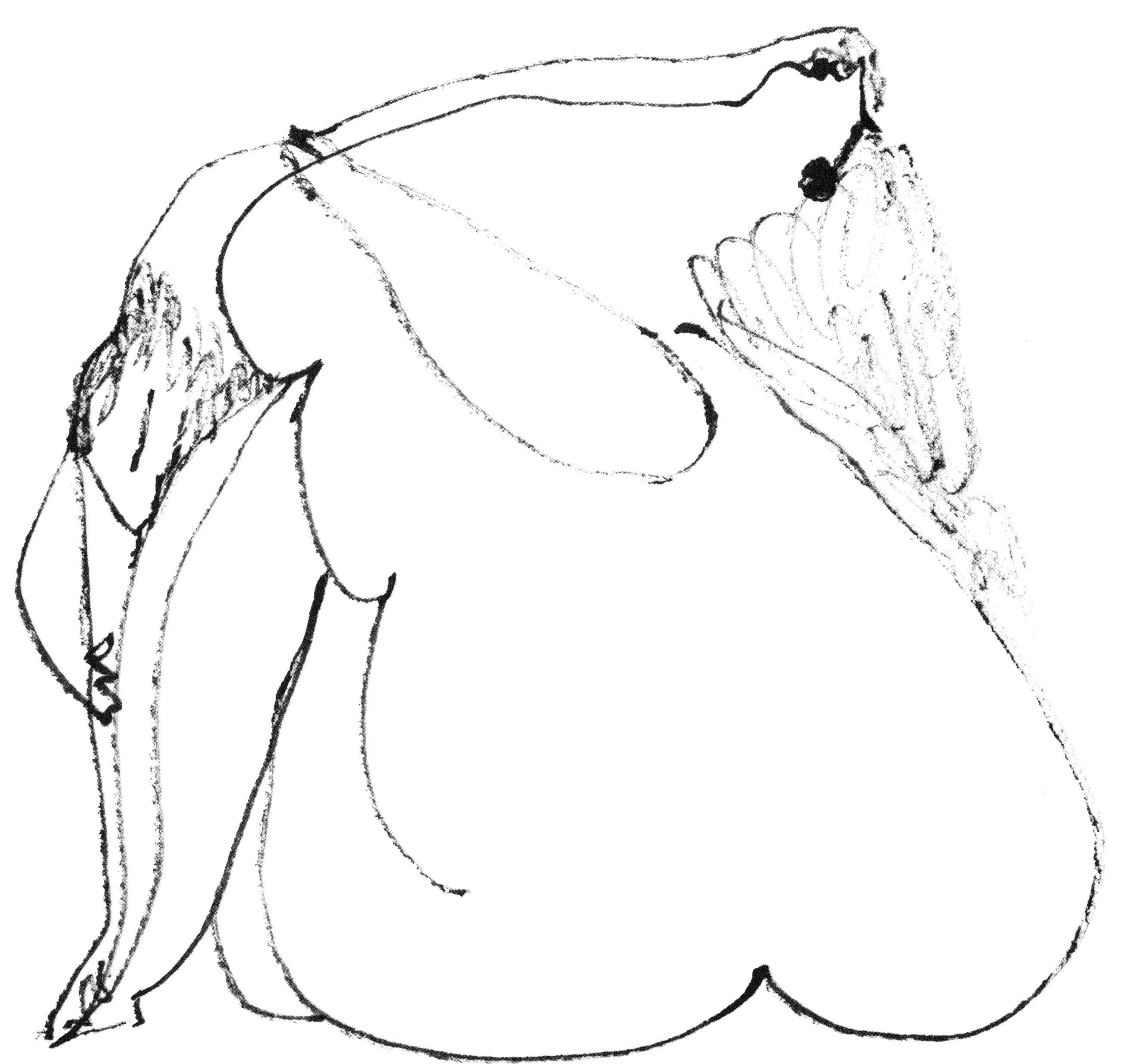

W. Steig

W. Steig

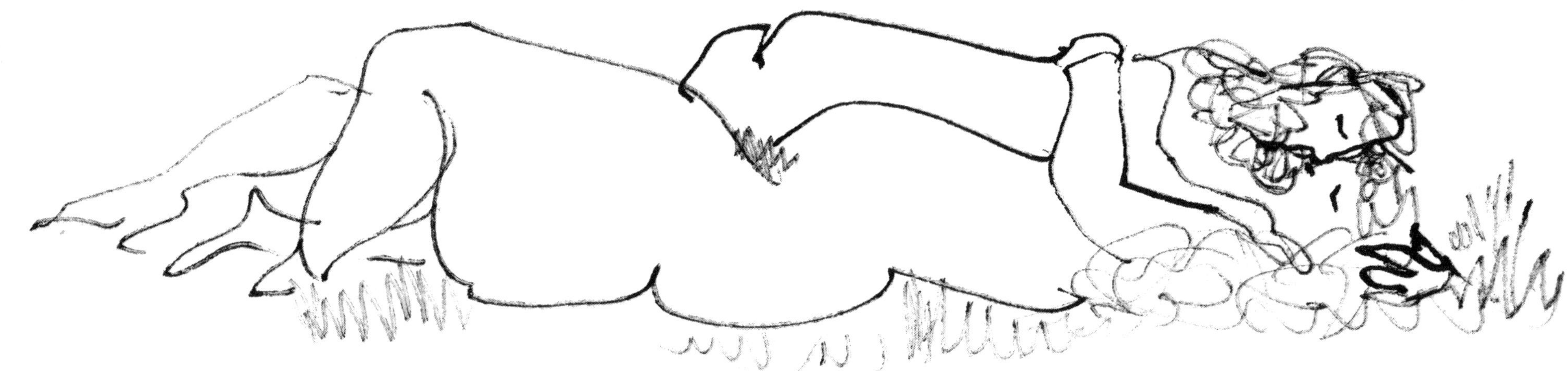

W. Steig

W.Steig

Steig

W. Steig

W. Steig

W. Steig

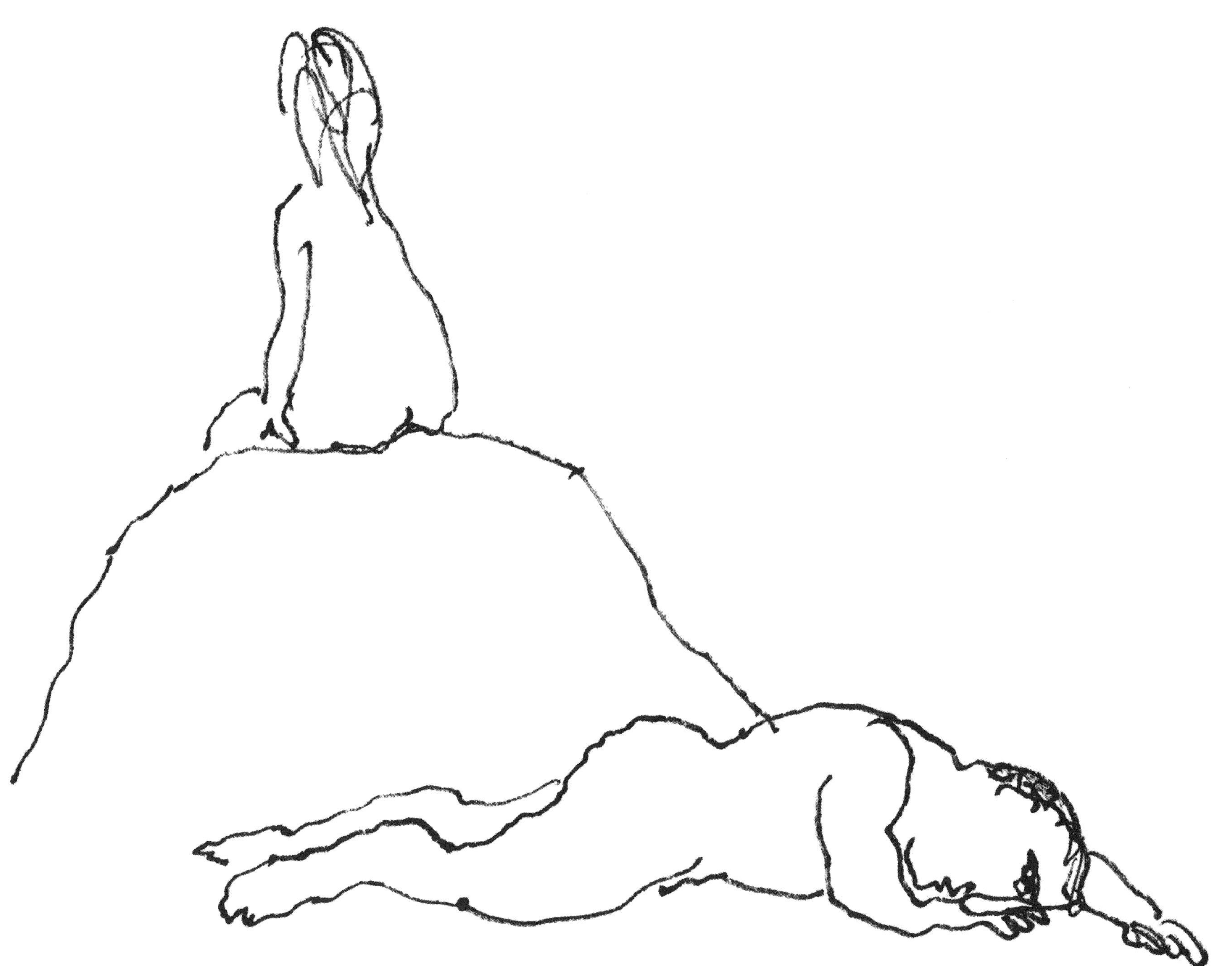

W. Steig

W. Steig

W. Steig

W. Steig

NO
W. Steig

W. Steig

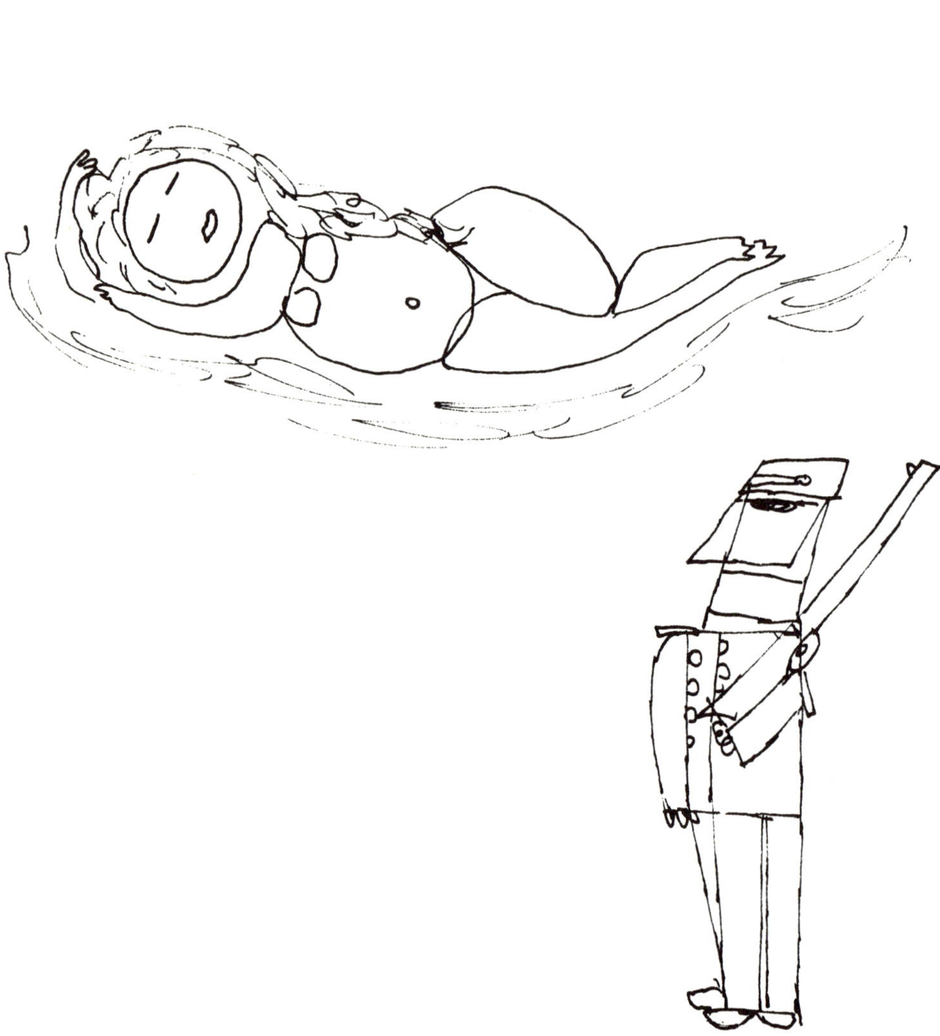

W. Steig

W. Steig

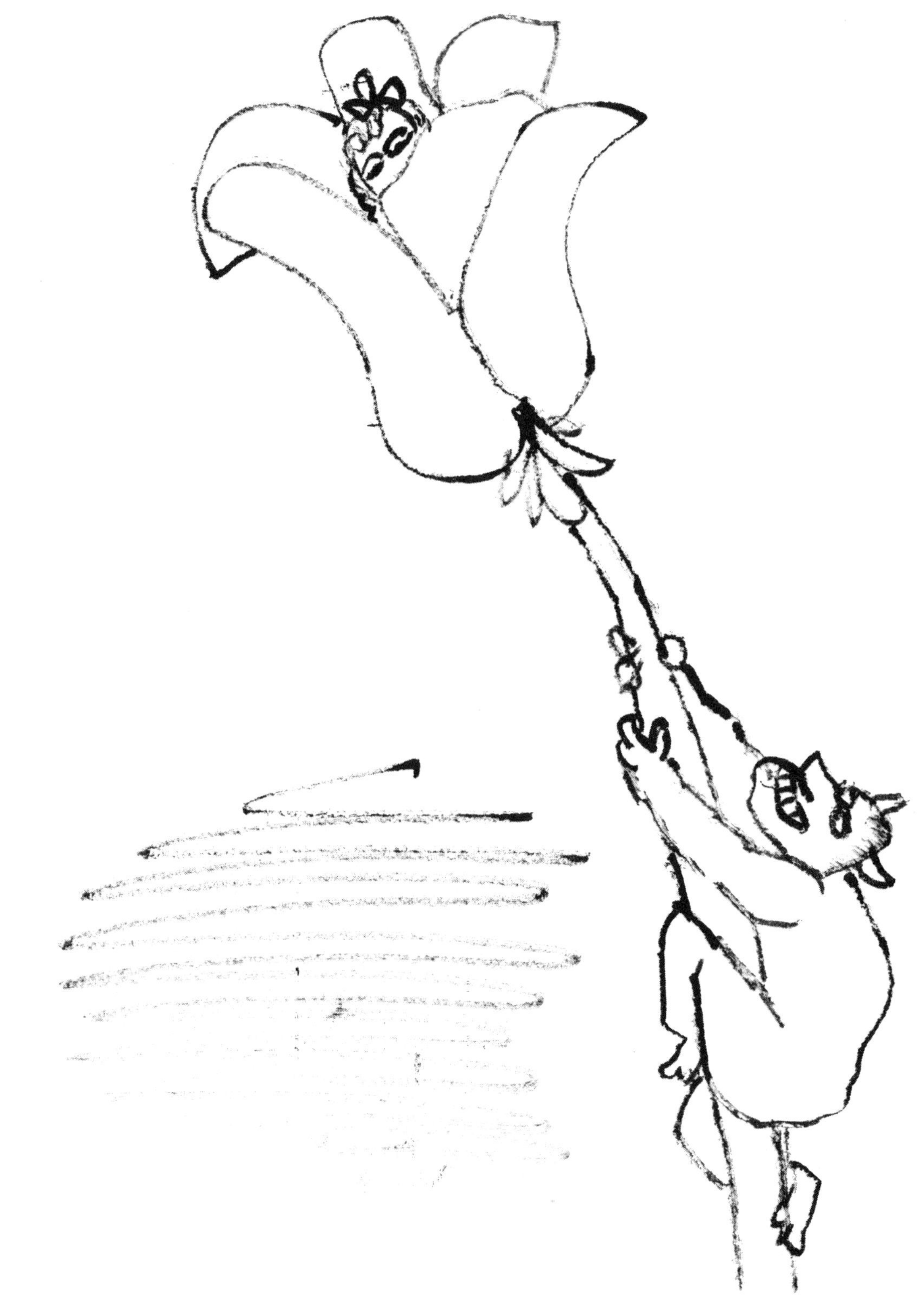